The Babysitter's Handbook

The Care and Keeping of Kids

by Harriet Brown
illustrations by Jodi Preston

★ American Girl®

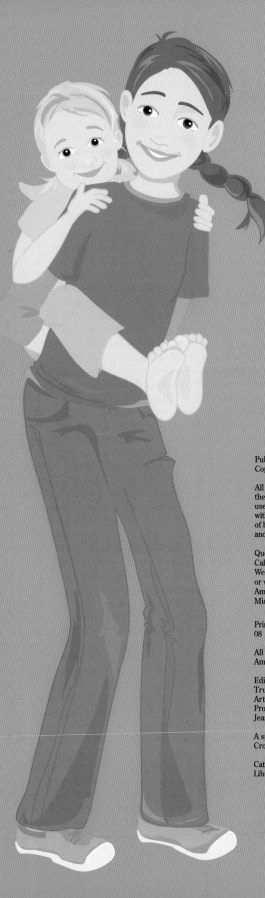

Published by American Girl Publishing, Inc.
Copyright © 1999, 2007 by American Girl, LLC.

Questions or comments?
Call 1-800-845-0005, visit our
Web site at **americangirl.com**,
or write to Customer Service,
American Girl, 8400 Fairway Place,
Middleton, WI 53562-0497.

Printed in China.
08 09 10 11 12 13 LEO 12 11 10 9 8 7

All American Girl marks are trademarks of
American Girl, LLC.

Editorial Development:
Trula Magruder, Michelle Watkins
Art Direction: Kym Abrams, Camela Decaire
Production: Kendra Schluter, Mindy Rappe,
Jeannette Bailey, Judith Lary

A special thanks to Molly Kelly, American Red
Cross, Badger Chapter

Cataloging-in-Publication Data available from the
Library of Congress

An important note to girls and parents:

The Babysitter's Handbook is designed to provide top-notch tips for caring for kids. What do you do when a child won't stop crying? How can you win over a shy six-year-old? What are the best games to play with babies? How do you handle a tantrum that goes on . . . and on . . . and on?

This handbook has the answers to these questions and much, much more—including tips and tricks from experienced babysitters.

But reading this book will *not* make you a certified babysitter. Books can't take the place of hands-on training—and books can't teach you everything you need to know about first aid and CPR. If you take this book on the job, the chapter on first aid will remind you what to do in an emergency—but it will not replace a first-aid class. To be certified, you must take a babysitter training course, like the one offered by the American Red Cross.

You need knowledge to care for children. So before bounding into the business of caring for kids, find out about babysitter training in your town, and sign up. Taking a course and reading books like this one will get you started. Before long, you'll have the confidence to tell your clients, "I am the best babysitter—ever!"

Your friends at American Girl

Contents

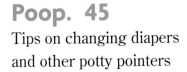

Whether you're a brand-new babysitter or an old pro, these questions and answers will give your skills and confidence a boost!

Babysitter Basics

What's the difference between a mother's helper and a babysitter?

A *mother's helper* entertains kids while the parents are at home—for instance, she might be inside with a child while a parent works in the garden. If a problem comes up, she can ask a parent for help. A *babysitter* cares for kids without an adult around. Since she has more responsibility, she gets paid more. Many sitters start out as mother's helpers because it's great practice.

How do I know if I'm ready to babysit?

There's no hard-and-fast rule. Some girls start to babysit when they're 14. Others start at 11. If you're not sure, ask yourself these questions: Do I feel responsible enough to care for kids? Can I handle discipline problems? Have I taken a Red Cross babysitting course? If you answered yes to these questions, you're ready to give babysitting a try.

I've never run a business before. How do I start?

Spread the word! Make flyers and hand them out to your parents' friends. If you have friends who babysit, let them know you're available. They may recommend you for jobs they're not free to take. Once you have a few customers, they'll spread the word for you. Before you take any job, discuss it with your parents. Make sure they know the family you'll be sitting for. Remember to write down the time the job starts and the address, even if you think you'll remember.

How much should I charge?

Most girls charge $4 to $8 an hour, depending on where they live and the number and ages of the kids they're sitting. Find out the going rate in your area. Ask friends what they charge. Ask neighbors what they pay. Some girls will take any pay a client offers. But it's best—for you and for your clients—if you set a fair price and tell the customer what you charge *before* you take the job.

Super Sitter Secret

A big plus

"I took a Red Cross babysitting course in my town. I recommend it for girls who want to be good babysitters. Plus, parents will be more apt to trust you with their kids if they know you're certified!"

Emily
Oregon

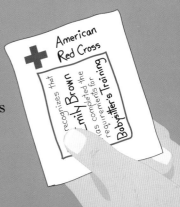

What if I change my mind?

How would you feel if you were set to do something fun and some-one said you couldn't? That's how parents feel when you cancel. If you're sick or a family emergency comes up, clients will under-stand. But if a friend calls you with ice show tickets on the day before a job, swallow hard and tell her you've made other plans. Your customers are counting on you.

How do I get there—and back home?

When you accept a job outside your neighborhood, let your clients know you'll need transportation. They'll get you there and back. If it's nighttime, make sure a grown-up walks or drives you home. But use your judgment. If for any reason at all you're nervous about someone taking you home, call your parents to come and get you.

What if I don't want to babysit?

If you're asked to babysit for kids you don't get along with, say something like, "I just don't think we're a good fit." Also, turn down jobs you don't think you can handle, such as caring for infant twins—especially if you've never babysat an infant.

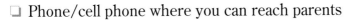

What do I need to know before the parents leave?

There's no such thing as too many questions—so ask parents *anything* you're not sure about! The first time you babysit, arrive a few minutes early and get the facts you need. The Client Address Book provided in the back of the kit is a great place to keep track of client information.

❏ Phone/cell phone where you can reach parents

❏ Address and phone number of house you're in

❏ Time parents expect to be home

❏ Name and phone number of a neighbor

❏ Name and phone number of children's doctor and hospital

❏ Nearest intersection of house where you're sitting

❏ Children's food and medicine allergies, if any

❏ What and when to feed children, including foods that are off-limits

❏ What to do with dirty diapers and clothes

❏ Bedtime and bedtime rituals for each child

❏ Snacks you can and can't eat

❏ Type of discipline to use if necessary (time-outs, no TV, etc.)

❏ Poison control center's number

❏ Emergency number

If I ask a lot of questions, won't the parents think I'm too inexperienced to babysit?

There isn't a question that will seem too dumb to parents. The more questions you ask, the smarter you'll seem. Parents will be thrilled that you know what to ask. After all, you're caring for the most important people in their lives. The more you know, the more confident you and your clients will be that you can handle anything that comes up.

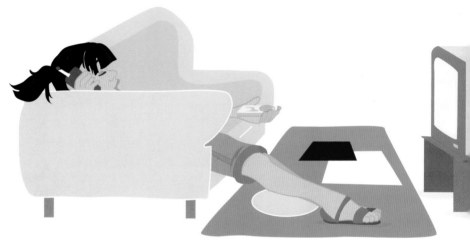

The parents told me to make myself at home. Can I?

A babysitter is not quite a guest and not quite a family member. But you should feel relaxed enough to take care of the children and yourself. If you're hungry, get yourself a snack. But don't make a mess, tie up the phone, or secretly invite friends over— these are just as rude at a client's house as they are at home. And never snoop! How would you feel if someone poked around your room while you were out? Respect a family's privacy the way you'd want others to respect yours.

What if I need help while I'm babysitting?

In a true emergency—for instance, if a child is seriously injured— call 911 and follow the directions given to you. This kind of situation is rare. But if a baby won't stop crying or a toddler locks himself in a room and you don't know what to do, just remember: Stay *calm* so the child will not be frightened. Keep a *cool* head so you can do what you're trained to do. And *call* your parents or the child's parents for help if you need it.

You've arrived on time and met the kids. You've gotten the list of last-minute instructions. Then Mom and Dad wave good-bye and close the door behind them—and the child bursts into tears. Now what?

Everything's O.K.!

Take a deep breath. These tears have nothing to do with you. It's normal for kids—especially little ones five and under—to get upset when their parents leave. These feelings even have a name: separation anxiety. With your help, most kids will cheer up pretty quickly once their parents are gone. Here's what you should do:

Reassure them . . .

Remind the child that his parents will be back in a little while. Even though he knows this, he may feel for a minute or two as if his parents will be gone *forever.* Just hearing the words "Don't worry, Mom and Dad will be home later" can help more than you think.

Or hold her hands and clap them together while you sing the words as a silly song: "Mommy goes away and Mommy comes back." It may sound corny to you, but it really does help.

You want kids to trust you, so always tell the truth about when their parents will return. Never promise a toddler that her parents will be back at bedtime if you don't expect them home until much later. If you know her parents will be home late, you could say something like, "When you wake up tomorrow morning, Mom and Dad will be right here at home."

. . . then distract them!

Some babysitters bring little treats for just this moment—a stick of gum for an older child, a colorful Band-Aid for a toddler. Other babysitters plan a special activity. These treats and games don't have to be fancy. They just have to help kids get over the "hump" of saying good-bye.

Offer a hug.

Settle the child into your lap with a favorite book.

Put on music and dance around together.

Offer a small treat, like a cookie.

Ask the child to show you her room.

Ask to see his toys.

Pull out a clean sock or pot holder to use as a puppet.

Ask about her pets.

Put on a video.

Pull out a pack of crayons and color.

If it's O.K. with the parents, take the child for a walk.

Say, "Whatever you do, don't smile!"

15

When the crying just won't stop . . .

You've tried every distraction you can think of and the child is still crying. Take a deep breath and stay calm. If a child is crying because her parents have just left, say something like, "Your mommy loves you very much. She and your dad are going to the movies. I know they'll miss you." It doesn't matter *what* you say—what you're really telling the child is that it's O.K. to feel sad for a while. She'll let you know when she's ready for fun.

But what if the crying *never* stops? If you've checked the diaper, tried to feed and soothe the child, and the crying continues, then it's time to get help. Babies and toddlers can't tell you what's wrong. They can't tell you if they're sick or in pain. So before you break into tears yourself, call your parents or the child's parents. They'll want to know what's going on. No one will get angry. Sometimes asking for help is the only thing you *can* do.

Mealtime Do's

Whether serving a snack or dinner, follow these basic rules to make mealtime a safe time.

Do make sure kids are safely occupied while you're preparing the meal.

Do check the temperature of the formula or milk. Shake a drop or two onto your wrist. If it feels hot to you, it's too hot for the baby.

Do have kids sit down at the table to eat.

Do feed kids only what parents have said is O.K.

Do cut food into small pieces. Round-shaped foods, like hot dogs and grapes, should be cut into half-circles so kids won't choke on them.

and Don'ts

Don't serve food that is too hot to eat. Make sure it has cooled off before you put it on the table.

 **Don't** leave leftovers out. Put them away in the fridge.

Don't walk away from a child who is eating—especially a baby. She can wriggle out of her chair and fall.

 **Don't** serve drinks in fragile glasses. Use plastic cups instead.

Don't leave dirty dishes on the table. Stack them in the sink.

I'm hungry.

Fun Food

Children can be picky eaters—remember when you wouldn't eat anything round or green? Your job is to serve them healthy snacks, not to fill them up with junk food. The key to feeding kids healthy food and keeping them happy is to make mealtime fun. Sound impossible? Try these tasty treats!

Bagel faces

Spread cream cheese over half a bagel. Use vegetable or fruit pieces to make hair, eyes, and a smile.

Cinnamon-sugar toast

Butter a slice of toast. Sprinkle a mixture of cinnamon and sugar over it. Cut off the crusts.

Sandwich shapes

Use cookie cutters to turn plain old PB and J into hearts, stars, and other dazzling designs.

Cracker sandwiches

Make cracker sandwiches with peanut butter, jelly, cream cheese, tuna salad, or sliced turkey.

Peewee pizzas

Spread tomato sauce onto an English muffin. Add cubes of cheese. Microwave on HIGH until the cheese melts. Let the child make a pizza face with cut vegetables.

Ants on a log

Spread peanut butter on a celery stick. Add a line of raisins.

Silly Servings

Sometimes *what* you feed kids isn't as important as *how* you feed them. A giggle or two can make everything taste better!

Have an indoor picnic

Spread a tablecloth or old sheet on the floor. Pack simple picnic food in lunch boxes or in a picnic basket. Pour juice or milk from a thermos.

Switcheroo

Let kids pretend they're the babysitters and you're the kid. Ask them to serve you—and themselves—a premade snack.

Play restaurant

Pretend the kids have come to a restaurant. You're the waitress (and cook!). Tell them "today's special." Write their orders on a notepad. While you're preparing the meal, give them paper and crayons. Let them know they have to "pay" for the meal with artwork!

I'm hungry.

Super Sitter Secret

Smooth sailing

"I like to make happy faces on sandwiches with raisins for the eyes and mouth. Or I stick a straw in the sandwich and tape on a paper sail for a sandwich boat!"

Robin
Vermont

Cleanup Time!

If there's one thing parents dislike, it's coming home to a messy kitchen. So make sure you clean up after yourself and the children. You don't have to wash every dish, but tidy up the kitchen the best you can. If you're caring for an infant, you won't have time to clean. That's O.K. Even grown-ups let chores slide when they're taking care of a baby!

Most kids enjoy helping with cleanup. Make up a silly song like "Clean up, clean up, everybody clean up!" or "Kristy is a helper, a helper, a helper. Kristy is a helper, yes she is." Choose chores that are right for each age. Toddlers and preschoolers can dry silverware and put it away. School-age kids can load the dishwasher or wash dishes. If you're not sure where something goes, ask. Kids love knowing more than you do.

Your Turn

I'm hungry!

You forgot to eat before you came to babysit, and now you're starving. What should you do?

No one wants you to starve. Help yourself to a small snack: cheese and crackers, a peanut butter sandwich, cookies and milk. But don't open foil-wrapped packages or dig through the freezer. Parents won't appreciate it if you eat tomorrow night's dinner!

Want to be everyone's favorite babysitter? Just remember these three little words: play with kids. What kids want most is your attention. Chances are, the kids you're babysitting will love anything you suggest—as long as you do it together.

Baby Play

Little ones need simple games. Be prepared to play them over and over!

Where's the ball?

Sit opposite baby on the floor. Gently roll a small ball toward her. Say something like, "Where's the ball? There it is! Can you roll it back to me?"

Which hand?

Put a small toy in one hand. Put both hands behind your back and ask baby to point to the hand that has the toy.

Look what I see!

Carry baby around the room, pointing out interesting objects—a vase of flowers, a ticking clock. Let her look out the window, and talk to her about what's outside: "Look, there's a tree with green leaves."

Want to sing?

Don't forget all those songs you learned as a child. Try singing "Itsy-Bitsy Spider," "I'm a Little Teapot," and "Head-Shoulders-Knees-and-Toes." And remember: It's all new to them!

See the animal?

Place stuffed animals throughout the house. Now walk baby through the house, pointing out and naming every animal you see: "Look, there's a bunny! I see a penguin. Do you see the kitty cat?"

Dance with me!

Put on some music and get moving! Babies love it when you spin them around. Don't do it right after a meal, and stop if you get dizzy.

Wanna play?

Super Sitter Secrets

Dress the part

"Don't wear necklaces or dangling earrings. Babies love to pull on them, and you could end up with sore ears or a broken necklace. Wear nice but comfortable clothes. You'll look professional and still be able to crawl around with the kids."

Melissa
Indiana

Justina
Arkansas

Toddler Time

Toddlers think everything's funny. The best games and activities for them are short and silly!

Color clues

Toddlers love to be right—especially when you're wrong! Sing, "Libby is a big girl, a big girl, a big girl. Libby is a big girl, and her shirt is blue!" Be sure to say the wrong color. The first few times you might have to correct yourself: "Blue? Noooooo, it's pink!" Soon *she'll* be correcting you!

Creative coloring

Make a one-of-a-kind coloring book. Fold three sheets of construction paper in half. Staple them together in the shape of a book. Draw pictures of the child, her parents, and her pets. Ask her to color them in.

Planet Purr

Pretend the sofa is a spaceship. With the child in your lap, lean left and right as the ship zooms into space. Once you "land," climb off onto Planet Purr, where everyone becomes a kitty! Get onto the ship to become human again.

Peewee pet care

For this emergency, you'll need a toy truck or car, strips of cloth, and a few stuffed animals. Ask the toddler to bandage the "injured" animals and transport them in the ambulance. Don't forget the siren!

Change machine

Drape a sheet over a table. Every time a child goes through the "change machine," she becomes something new—firefighter, frisky puppy, or ballerina!

Around town

Turn cardboard boxes into a town. Get out toy cars and as many "people" as you can find.

Wanna play?

27

Kid Games

Older kids have their own ideas of how to have fun. Offer these when they're ready for something new.

Basketball

Crumple pieces of newspaper to make ten balls for each kid. Set out a trash can. Each child tries to make as many baskets as possible.

Letter writing

Ask kids to "send" you letters, describing what they want to do the next time you babysit. Let them seal the letters in envelopes and drop them into a "mailbox" or "mailbag" you've set out. Read them when you get home!

Card games

Bring a deck of cards, and show kids a new game each time you babysit. In Concentration, lay out all the cards facedown. Take turns flipping over two cards. If the numbers match, pick up the cards and take another turn. At the end, the one with the most cards wins!

Magazine scavenger hunt

Give each child an old magazine or catalog, along with a list of things to find, cut out, and glue onto paper.

Soft volleyball

Run a piece of string across the floor, and have kids stand on either side. Blow up a balloon. Toss it back and forth without letting it touch the ground.

Junior babysitter

Kids love coming up with games for the little ones. Put them in charge of creating activities for toddlers or babies. Be sure to play the games with them!

Super Sitter Secret

Clean queen

"One time I was babysitting four little girls. They were bored, and the house was a mess. So I invented a game. In each room, a girl was the queen and the rest of us were servants. She told us what to pick up or clean. We appointed a new queen for each room. It worked like a charm, and their mom was happy about the house!"

Anna
Washington

Wanna play?

Pack Up!

Kids will get a kick out of anything you bring along. Your goodies don't have to be new—they'll be new to the kids, and that's all that matters.

❏ Children's video, DVD, or music CD

❏ Colorful Band-Aids

❏ Toys (but not tiny toys; try trucks, dolls, etc.)

❏ Stuffed animal

❏ Puppets (can be made from socks or pot holders)

❏ Bubbles

❏ Stickers

❏ Board game

❏ Playing cards

❏ Children's books

❏ Old catalogs or magazines

❏ Paper and envelopes

❏ Coloring books and crayons

31

Uh-oh. The kids have been arguing—and arguing—all evening. You feel more like a referee than a babysitter! How can you stop the squabbling?

Cool Them Off

First, make sure the kids don't hurt each other, and give everyone a little time to settle down. Put the children in different rooms, or in opposite corners of the same room. Tell them, "We're all going to take a time-out for five minutes." Set a timer, and make sure everybody's quiet until it rings.

Talk it out

Many arguments aren't about anything important—they're the way kids let off steam at one another. But when real conflicts do come up, it's your job to help sort things out.

The best way to do that is to have the kids talk to each other. Stand one on either side of you, facing each other. Give each child two minutes to express her feelings, one at a time. A few important rules: The kids must talk to each other, not to you. They must talk about their own feelings, not just rehash what the other one said or did. And they must really listen to what the other child says.

Once both kids have aired their feelings, the argument may be over. But if the kids are still fighting, you have to help them work it out. Ask each of them to offer a fair solution to the problem. If they can't come up with a plan they both like, offer a compromise. If the argument is over a doll, for instance, you might suggest that each child take a five-minute turn with the doll. Or point out another doll that could be added to the game.

If the kids just can't agree, let them know that you will solve the problem your way—by taking away the toy or ending the game. Give them one more chance to work it out, and then do what you said you would.

Super Sitter Secret

Funny face

"When kids are fighting, I set them on chairs across from each other and tell them to give each other ugly faces. Before you know it, they can't frown, and they end up laughing!"

Jen
Wisconsin

She hit me!

I'm Telling!

Kids tell on each other for two reasons.

They can't solve the problem

Help kids talk to each other to try to resolve the problem themselves. If they can't, *you* make a decision—and make sure everyone sticks to it.

They want your attention

Play with the kids. If they don't want you to play, stay close enough to hear what's going on. Let them know you're around. They'll be glad, even if they don't seem to care. If they're still tattling, say, "I won't listen to tattling, but I *will* listen if you want to tell me how *you* feel or about something *you* did."

Super Sitter Secret

A happy medium

"While I was babysitting, one kid wanted to watch *Little Women* and the other wanted to watch *Toy Story*. I asked them to decide on their own, then went to fix popcorn. When I came back, the kids had agreed to *Little Women* because they had seen *Toy Story* once already."

Carly
Wisconsin

34